Jane and the Jay

Written by Alison Hawes

Illustrated by Wendy Sinclair

It was Saturday and Jane was playing
shops in her garden.

"Today, I am Mrs May the shopkeeper," said Jane, as she set up her shop.

"I have eighteen things for sale," Jane said, as she set out the display in her shop.

Up in a tree, a jay spotted a big red ring on Jane's tray.

Then it began to rain. "Oh no!" said Jane. "My display will get wet!"

Jane took her hat and made her way down the road.

"I will stay in until the rain stops,"
she said.

When Jane was away, the jay
came down from the tree to take
a look at the rings in her shop.

"I will take this ring for Mrs Jay,"
he said.

But Jane had seen the jay take the ring.
"That is no way to behave, Mr Jay!"
Jane said.

"Customers must not take things from a shop," she had to explain. "They have to pay!"

"Oh no!" said Mr Jay. "I made a
mistake. I forgot to pay."

So he came down from the tree right
away and gave Jane a coin.